A NOTE TO PARENTS

When your children are ready to "step into reading," giving them the right books—and lots of them—is as crucial as giving them the right food to eat. **Step into Reading Books** present exciting stories and information reinforced with lively, colorful illustrations that make learning to read fun, satisfying, and worthwhile. They are priced so that acquiring an entire library of them is affordable. And they are beginning readers with an important difference—they're written on four levels.

Step 1 Books, with their very large type and extremely simple vocabulary, have been created for the very youngest readers. **Step 2 Books** are both longer and slightly more difficult. **Step 3 Books,** written to mid-second-grade reading levels, are for the child who has acquired even greater reading skills. **Step 4 Books** offer exciting nonfiction for the increasingly proficient reader.

Children develop at different ages. **Step into Reading Books,** with their four levels of reading, are designed to help children become good—and interested—readers *faster*. The grade levels assigned to the four steps—preschool through grade 1 for Step 1, grades 1 through 3 for Step 2, grades 2 and 3 for Step 3, and grades 2 through 4 for Step 4—are intended only as guides. Some children move through all four steps very rapidly; others climb the steps over a period of several years. These books will help your child "step into reading" in style!

Text copyright © 1992 by Joyce Milton. Illustrations copyright © 1992 by Larry Schwinger. All rights reserved under International and Pan-American Copyright Conventions. Published in the United States by Random House, Inc., New York, and simultaneously in Canada by Random House of Canada Limited, Toronto.

Library of Congress Cataloging-in-Publication Data:
Wild, wild wolves / by Joyce Milton; illustrated by Larry Schwinger.
p.   cm.–(Step into Reading. Step 2 book.)
Summary: Introduces the natural history of wolves, examining their social structure, hunting tactics, growth, and development, and explores myths and legends about them.
ISBN: 0-679-81052-8 (pbk.) – 0-679-91052-2 (lib. bdg.) 1. Wolves–Juvenile literature. [1. Wolves.] I. Schwinger, Larry, ill. II. Title. III. Series.
QL737.C22M56   1992   599.74′442–dc20   90-8807

Manufactured in the United States of America   10

STEP INTO READING is a trademark of Random House, Inc.

Step into Reading

Wild, Wild WOLVES

By Joyce Milton
Illustrated by Larry Schwinger

A Step 2 Book

Random House 🏠 New York

On a summer night

in the far north

a wolf is howling.

"OW-OOO!

OW-OOO!"

One by one, all the wolves

for miles around

throw back their heads

and join in—

"OW-OW-OW-OWOOO!"

Miles away,
a family camping
near a big lake
hears the howls.
The children grab
their parents' hands.

Nothing sounds

as wild and scary

as a howling wolf!

Do wolves howl

just before they attack?

No!

To a wolf, a howl

is a friendly sound.

Wolves howl to let other wolves

know where they are.

They may even howl

just for fun.

Sometimes a pet dog

throws back its head and howls.

It sounds just like a wolf!

That is because wolves and dogs

are close relatives.

Long, long ago,

when people lived in caves,

some wolves began

to wait nearby

for the scraps of meat

that people threw away.

Cave children

played with the wolf pups.

Little by little,

the wolves became tame.

These tame wolves
were the first pets.
Every dog on earth today—
from tiny toy poodles
to big St. Bernards—
is related to them.

A few people still try

to tame wolves.

Eskimos have trained them

to pull dogsleds.

But a wolf

is not a house pet.

To be happy,

it must be wild and free.

A wolf's long legs

are made for running—

up to 40 miles in a single day!

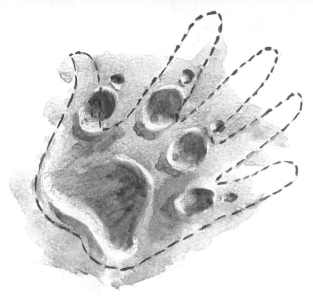

Its huge paws can be
as large as a grownup's hand.
Its powerful jaws can crack
the leg bone of a moose
with a single snap.

Wolves are hunters.
To stay alive,
they need fresh meat—
lots of it.

A hungry wolf can eat
20 pounds of meat
at a single meal.
That's like eating
one hundred hamburgers!
To get all this meat,
wolves usually hunt big animals
like deer and moose.
But a hungry wolf
will chase and eat
a rabbit or a mouse.

It may even go fishing!

Wolves live in groups
called packs.
The pack members
"talk" to each other
with their bodies.
When a wolf is scared,
it holds its ears
close to its head.
When a wolf is happy,
it wags its whole tail.
If it wags just the tip,
watch out!
It is getting ready to attack.

Other wolves know these signals.
The signals help the wolves
live together without fighting.

Every pack has a lead male

and a lead female.

The lead male is strong and smart.

He will fight any wolf

that tries to take over his pack.

The lead female

is usually the mother

of the pack's cubs.

The lead male

shows he is the boss

by the way he acts.

He looks the other wolves

right in the eye.

The other wolves tuck their tails
between their legs.
They rub noses with the leader
and lick his face.

In the spring

the lead female

gets ready to have pups.

She digs a den

in the side of a hill.

The other wolves help her.

The pups are born

in early May.

Their eyes are closed.

They cannot see or hear.

They live by drinking

their mother's milk.

In three weeks

the pups are big enough

to leave the den.

At first they are afraid.

But soon they are racing

up and down the hillside,

playing tag.

One pup sees a grasshopper.

She pounces—SWOOSH!

But the grasshopper gets away.

The pup looks surprised.

She tries again. And again.

This is the little wolf's

first lesson in hunting.

The adult wolves

take turns baby-sitting.

While the father

guards the pups,

they tug on his tail

and nip at his ears.

If they are too rough,

he just gets up and walks away.

The pups roll around,

pretending to fight.

One of them is stronger

than her sisters and brothers.

She holds her tail high.

She is already acting

like a lead wolf.

The pups are hungry
all the time.
When the older wolves
go hunting,
they chew extra food
and swallow it.
Back at the den,
they spit up the
chewed food—
and the hungry pups
get their first taste of meat!

By September the pups

are half-grown.

They spend hours chasing mice,

but they don't catch any.

They are too slow and clumsy.

But soon the pups will

hunt along with the pack.

In six months

they will be good hunters.

One cold November morning
the wolves smell moose nearby.
The pack moves out
in single file
across the snow.

The wolves chase many moose.

Most of them run away.

But one big moose

stands and fights.

It kicks out

with its powerful hooves.

An angry moose can kill a wolf.

Soon the pack leaves it alone.

Finally, the wolves

find an old, sick moose.

It is too weak

to run or fight.

The pack fans out in a circle.

One wolf charges.

It bites the moose's nose

and hangs on tight.

In minutes the fight is over.

The hungry wolves can eat.

A wolf hunting alone

might never catch a large animal.

Hunting in packs

helps all the wolves to survive.

Many people

have never seen a live wolf.

The only wolves they meet

are in fairy tales

and horror movies.

Fairy tale wolves

are greedy and dangerous.

The scariest of all

make-believe wolves

is the werewolf.

By day the werewolf

is an ordinary man or woman.

But at night,

when the moon is full,

the werewolf's teeth

become long and sharp.

Hair grows on its face.

It runs on all fours—

just like a real wolf.

The werewolf

roams the moonlit forest

and attacks anyone it meets!

Legends about killer wolves

made many people believe

that wolves were their enemies.

For a long time

hunters shot every wolf

they could find.

They even shot wolves

from airplanes.

At last some scientists
began to wonder if wolves
really were so dangerous.
They went deep into the forest
to study how wolves live.

One scientist

was walking in the forest

when he met two wolves

by accident.

One wolf ran away.

The other wolf

walked right up to him.

The scientist was scared.

But the wolf

just licked his face

and trotted away!

The scientists learned
that healthy wolves
do not attack people.
But when wolves
wander onto farms,
they soon learn
that a lamb or a calf
makes a good dinner.
Some farmers use sheepdogs
to scare away wolves.

Some kill wolves

with poison, traps, or guns.

The American Indians

did not fear wolves.

They admired the way

wolves lived in peace together.

The Sioux Indians

told the story of a woman

who got lost in a snowstorm.

A wolf pack saved her life.

The wolves brought her food.

They let her sleep in their den.

They taught her their secrets.

When the woman

went back to her own people,

she taught them

the secrets of the wolves.

She became a powerful magician.

A few hundred years ago

wolves lived all around the world.

Thousands of wolves

lived in North America.

Areas in red and black show where wolves once roamed. Areas in black show where wolves can be found today.

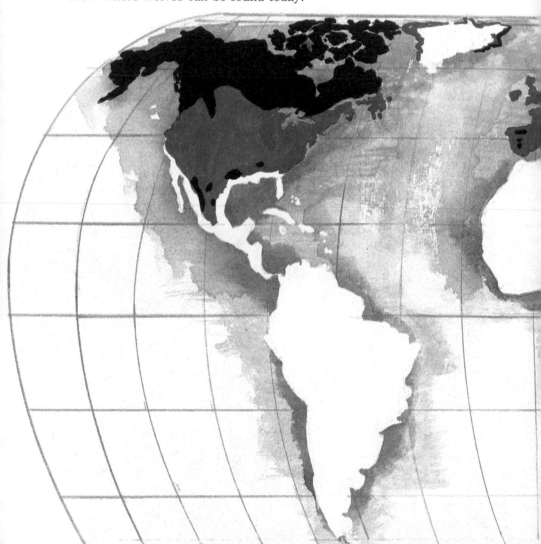

Today there are many more people
and fewer wolves.
In most of the United States
there are no wolves left at all
except in zoos.

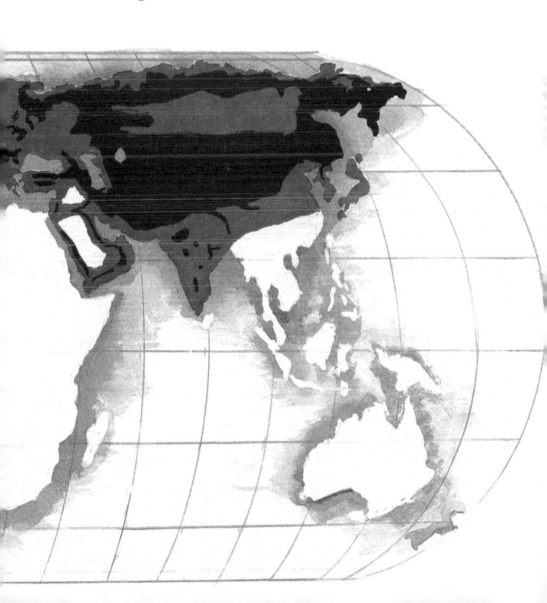

Wolves don't cause pollution.

They live without

hurting the land.

The pack hunts to survive.

There are always

moose and deer left

to have next spring's babies.

Today people are trying

to live in tune with nature,

as wolves do.

They want to save

some of the wild places

left on earth.

If that happens,

there will be

wild, wild wolves

howling in the forests

for years to come.